Some Bugs Buzz

By Carmel Reilly

T0342848

This is Mazz.

Her job is to look at bugs.

Mazz will tell us some bug stuff!

Bugs are fab!

Some bugs buzz.

They buzz as they zip
to the buds.

This bug can not buzz,
but it has lots of fuzz on it.

fuzz

This is **not** a bug.

It has no fuzz.

And it can not see!

Some bugs have dull shells.

But this bug's shell
has gloss on top.

This bug gets very still.

It looks stiff.

This red bug is not stiff!

It hops on and off moss.

CHECKING FOR MEANING

1. What 'bug stuff' did Mazz tell the reader? *(Literal)*

2. When do bugs buzz? *(Literal)*

3. Why do bugs get in fizz? *(Inferential)*

EXTENDING VOCABULARY

dull	What is the meaning of *dull* in this text? Why might some shells be dull?
stiff	What does it mean when something is *stiff*? What is another word in the book that has a similar meaning? I.e. *still*.
moss	What is *moss*? What colour is it? How does it grow?

MOVING BEYOND THE TEXT

1. What are some of the bugs you see near your home?

2. How is the body of a bug made up?

3. What do bugs eat?

4. How do bugs stay safe from predators?

SPEED SOUNDS

ff	ll	ss	zz

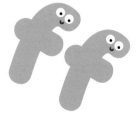

PRACTICE WORDS

will

Mazz

tell

buzz

shells

stuff

fuzz

stiff

gloss

dull

off

Off

moss

still

fizz

shell